From Sorrow to Dancing

How to Move Through Loss into the Rest of Your Life

By
Marcy Kelly

Edited by
Tammy Barley

xulon PRESS

Dedication

To Jayme and Glenn

Thank you both for your love and support.

Contents

Preface

Their eyebrows usually go up as their eyes get wide and they say something like, "Oh." That's what happens when I tell someone that I have been widowed twice. All of a sudden, whatever their impression of me was before, it is different now. Some have said, "You are so young," or "That must have been terrible." I immediately reassure them with, "It's okay and I've come through it." Coming through grief with its pain and confusion isn't easy but it can be done.

This book is for the widow who wants to know how to go on now that her life has changed. God walked me through my pain and I want to tell others how and why I did not get "stuck" in widowhood.

In preparation for the book, I interviewed widows to understand how others have handled their grief. Each widow has given permission to use her story. I changed the name of each one, and of her husband, to protect their identities.

As I interviewed them, they graciously thought back to the difficult days after their husbands died. Tears often came as each one relived the most difficult time in her life. To each woman who allowed me to write her story, I say "Thank you." Each widow felt the pain again so that you, the reader, might understand that you are not alone. Someone has walked the path before you and others will come behind. By walking this well-worn path with a sister, you too can walk through the grief into the rest of your life.

Marcy Kelly
January 1, 2008

Chapter One

From Sorrow to Dancing

Young girls pretend to be all sorts of things. They pretend to be Cinderella, a wife, a mommy, a teacher, a nurse, a doctor, a secretary, or a model, but they never pretend to be a widow. I used to think of a widow as someone who wore black, was sad, old, slumped over, and looked like the witch from *Hansel and Gretel*. Even when I did not see her as a witch, a widow was certainly something that I did not want to be. God's plan includes roles we want to play and some we would never choose for ourselves. God's plan for me included being wonderful things like a mother, a wife, a daughter, a sister, and a ballroom dancer. However, His plan also included being a widow. I was widowed by cancer twice before I was fifty-two.

How it all Started

I am an identical twin. My sister, Cindy, and I were born seventeen minutes apart. As children and teens, I always felt that I walked in her shadow. Although being in her shadow allowed me to feel a little more secure, fear has dominated my life. During most of my life I didn't even realize fear was guiding my steps. However, fear of disappointing others, fear of not being good enough, and many other fears have always been just under the surface of my confident façade.

The Empty House

When we were in second grade, Cindy and I were walking home from the school bus when our six-year-old friend came running out of her house screaming and crying that there was no furniture in her house. We went into the house with her and found it was completely empty. Her parents had moved everything out while she was at school. We all thought she had been abandoned. Although her parents drove up a few minutes after we finished searching the house, the trauma of being six years old and trying to help another six-year-old cope with abandonment lingered in my mind.

When we were ten, our family relocated to Alabama so my father could get a better job. Since we were living in a house that our parents intended to stay in temporarily, all the moving boxes were left unopened and piled to make a divider between our living room and dining table. Daddy later referred to this time as "camping out." I never felt secure in that house. I was afraid my parents might move away while I was at school and I might come home to find an empty house like my friend had a couple of years before.

Fear of what I would do if I came home one day and found our house empty crouched inside my mind daily. Could I also be abandoned? What would stop my parents from doing what my friend's parents had done?

Although I never understood or communicated the fear to my parents, I felt so frightened that fitting in at school was hard. I was also afraid Cindy and I would be separated at school. My security was in being in my sister's shadow and being one of two. Before I could really feel secure in Alabama, we moved to Houston, Texas.

Security and Fun

Houston was a big city. Even though our parents again bought a temporary house to live in until we found one we wanted, we did unpack. The street we lived on had several families with children our age. We began to make friends and fit into the new city.

We found it was possible to become dancers on a local TV dance show called *The Larry Kane Show*. Everyone who danced on the show was required to take weekly ballroom dancing lessons. We learned West Coast and East Coast Swing, Cha-cha, Mambo, Fox-trot and other dances. Following a ballroom dancing partner came easily to me. After all, I was used to following my twin.

Cindy and I not only loved dancing, we loved the special attention we received as twins on the TV show. We even received fan mail. Going to dance class and dancing on the show was wonderful. Our lives were filled with football games, pep club activities, homework, dancing, acting in the school play, and hanging out with friends. We trusted that life would continue to be secure; we would each go to college, get married, have families, and continue life on the day-to-day level we were currently living.

As I was looking toward a secure future in Texas, my parents began talking about moving back to the East Coast as soon as we graduated from high school.

Graduate, Move, Start College

Three days after high school graduation, our family moved from our ideal setting in Houston to Maryland. Our parents said we were moving to be closer to our grandparents, but that was not the underlying reason. I was unaware that they planned to divorce as soon as Cindy and I were settled into college. I had never heard my parents fight and had no idea that they weren't happily married.

When they sat us down in the living room to tell us they were getting a divorce, I felt shocked and frightened at what my future would hold. My world was falling apart. First, we had moved from our ideal life in Houston. Now my parents were dissolving our family unit. What would be next?

Out of Her Shadow

In September, without having visited even one college campus, Cindy went to a college in western Maryland and I went to Towson University near Baltimore. Cindy and I were hundreds of miles apart in a day when long-distance calls were very expensive and cell phones didn't exist. This was the first time Cindy and I had ever been separated. Separation from my sister rocked my world even further.

My first semester at college was very difficult. I felt lonely but was never alone as there was no privacy in the dorm. I had moved from a very quiet family where I encountered very little conversation to a dorm room with three girls who never stopped talking. Even the shower was a public place. All the girls on our floor shared one large shower. There seemed to be nowhere I could find peace and quiet.

On the first day at the dorm, all female students were told that if we returned to the dorm after nine thirty on weeknights or after midnight on the weekends, we would be given demerits and have to go before a disciplinary board. As a nervous rule-follower, if I went to the library to study or tried to find peace and quiet outside the dorm, I looked at my watch so often that I lost my concentration. I couldn't study, I couldn't sleep, and I didn't fit in. My personal world had fallen apart, and now my educational world was in a shambles.

The general fear and insecurity continued. I was so upset that I could not even finish my final exams while living in the dorm. Due to stress, I became ill and had to return home. Once at home, I again felt safe and was able to study. To complete the semester, I commuted to school to take each final exam. My grades were good enough to allow me to be on the Dean's List, but my insecurity and internal fears did not allow me to return to Towson as a student. This National Honor Society member and cum laude high school graduate had lasted one semester at college. I had no goals, no idea of my abilities, and no career path to follow.

Neal Enters My Life

It has been said that if you have no idea where you are going, any path will take you there. So, after a few months of looking for a job, I took a personnel receptionist job where I met a man who would greatly influence the course of my future. That man was Neal A. Block. Neal was divorced, good looking, well spoken, successful, thirteen years older than me, and an authority figure.

One day, Neal came to my desk and said that he was about to launch a coup to take me from the receptionist desk to being his secretary. Although he never asked if I wanted to be his secretary, the transfer was made. As we worked together, we began to be attracted to each other and started dating. He took me out for wonderful dinners, and I enjoyed being on the arm of someone who knew where he was going in life. I felt secure and unafraid with Neal.

Neal was Jewish and I was a Christian. Since I had never had any Jewish friends, I did not know that the Jewish religion was any different from the Christian religion. Although I had become a Christian at the age of seven, I had not gone to church or Sunday school very often and had no real understanding of what being a follower of Jesus really meant. The thought of being married was exciting and I was eager to adopt Neal's Jewish traditions. Again, I was walking in someone's shadow rather than being my own person.

As an engaged couple with different faiths, we had a difficult time finding someone who would marry us. We couldn't be married in a church or a synagogue. We didn't fit anywhere. We finally found a rabbi who would perform the ceremony even though I was not Jewish. Neal and I were married by a liberal rabbi under a canopy in the social hall of my apartment complex. We were surrounded by family and friends. I wore a beautiful but simple white bridal gown made by my mother's best childhood friend, Betty.

Although we had many cultural differences, Neal and I got along pretty well for five years during which time we didn't practice either religion. When we were dating, I had promised Neal that I would rear our children in the Jewish faith. I did not realize what that meant until I became pregnant.

Jewish tradition suggests that babies should be named for a deceased relative. Neal wanted our baby, if it was a boy, to be named after his deceased father, Edward Allen Block. I initially agreed. However, as I came closer to delivering the baby, I realized that I did not feel comfortable with the baby's first name being Edward. I started looking at other names in a baby book and ran across the name Jamie with spellings of Jayme and Jaime.

Betty, my mother's friend who had made my wedding dress, had a son named Jamie. Betty and her husband, Jim, had meant so much to me throughout my life that I thought naming a child Jayme was appropriate. Neal agreed, and we compromised by naming our child Jayme Edward.

The next morning after deciding on the baby's name, I went into labor. After three intense hours, Jayme was born. Jayme was a wonderful baby and a well-behaved, busy child. I enjoyed sharing him with his grandparents and was pleased to be able to be a stay-at-home mom during most of Jayme's early years.

Although I never converted to Judaism, true to my promise, I took Jayme to a reformed synagogue to learn Hebrew and about his Jewish roots. I became active at the synagogue as the person who visited elderly Jewish nursing home residents. Jayme and I took Jewish holiday celebrations to the local nursing homes. I was the liaison between the nursing homes and the synagogue. For several years Neal, Jayme, and I lived a comfortable life in the reformed Jewish community.

In mid-May 1984, Jayme was finishing fourth grade, Neal had just been promoted to vice president of his company, and I had gone back to college. I was finally feeling confident and secure.

Then Neal was diagnosed with lung cancer. The diagnosis came after a routine physical where the doctor noticed a hard lump on Neal's right shoulder. The lump was removed and biopsied. Initially, the doctor said the lump looked benign (non-cancerous), so I did not go with Neal to the follow-up appointment. I have always regretted that Neal was alone when the doctor told him that the lump was cancerous.

Neal was upset when he arrived home from the doctor's office. As he put his keys on the kitchen table, he told me he had cancer. A thousand questions and emotions went through my mind. There were very few answers that day since Neal had been given the diagnosis with no explanation. I was in shock, angry, sad, and felt I had to "fix it" right away. We had to pick an oncologist (cancer doctor) and see him as soon as possible. I immediately jumped into my problem-solver mode, but my efforts were delayed because we were coming into the Memorial Day weekend. It was the longest holiday I have ever experienced.

Three Months of Cancer Treatment

We spent Memorial Day knowing that Neal had cancer but not knowing what type of cancer, who would treat him, if he would be healed or die, how long he would live, what our lives would be like while he lived with cancer, or how Jayme and I would be supported after Neal died. On and on the questions went. I was sad and frightened.

But most of all, I was angry at Neal for putting us into this situation. I was a thirty-four-year-old mom. I had a nine-year-old son and a forty-seven-year-old husband who had terminal lung cancer because of a choice he had made to smoke three cartons, 600 individual cigarettes, per week. At that time, I was working at a low-paying, part-time job and was going to a local community college in pursuit of an associate's degree in computer science. I had no idea how Jayme and I would handle life if Neal became so sick that he couldn't work, let alone what we would do if Neal died. I felt as though I wanted to run in *any* direction, but there were so many things in my life that I couldn't control that I also felt paralyzed.

I simply had to make myself take things fifteen minutes at a time. I planned my day one task at a time because that was as far as I could think. I spent a lot of time on the phone updating caring friends and relatives about Neal's condition. Many days I wished there were a recording that I could play for that day's update rather than having to rehash each detail and listen to advice.

During our first visit, the oncologist said Neal would probably live three to five years but there was no cure for his type of lung cancer. Despite the fact that the cancer was incurable, the oncologist set up chemotherapy and radiation treatments for Neal.

In the beginning, Neal continued working. Then, one day in June, Neal was confused about how to get to work. As he drove away from our neighborhood, he realized that he did not know where he was going, so he turned around and came home. He called me at work and said that I needed to come home immediately.

When I arrived at home, I found the car in the driveway with the driver's door open, the front door to the house open, and Neal sitting in the family room looking very frightened. He told me what had happened. I immediately called the oncologist.

I had to be very assertive to get the oncologist to do more tests. After a long discussion, the doctor ordered a CAT scan of Neal's brain. The CAT scan showed between five and eight small brain tumors. When the doctor saw the CAT scan, he told me that Neal would live much less than three years. Neal actually lived only three months after the initial diagnosis. He received the diagnosis in mid-May, 1984 and died September 13, 1984.

During the summer of Neal's illness, while our lives were falling apart, Neal, Jayme, and I spoke with a therapist whose specialty was counseling in death and dying. She suggested that, as a family, we should read the Elisabeth Kubler-Ross books on death and dying. That summer, the three of us spent many hours on our screened-in deck as I read aloud about death and dying. Although it might seem like a very hard subject for a nine-year-old boy to learn about, I have always been glad that we allowed Jayme to be part of the discussions and readings. I believe it helped him to feel a little more confident that he and I would be all right when Neal was gone. Jayme also learned that his emotions were normal.

One day as we sat on the back deck, Jayme asked Neal what would happen to me after Neal died. With tears in his eyes, Neal said the most wonderful thing he had ever said during our marriage. He said he hoped that one day some nice man would marry mommy and be a good father to

Jayme. That one statement was of utmost importance in my decision to remarry after Neal's death.

September 13, 1984 was the day my nine-year-old son and I began the next part of the journey in God's plan. God had been providing for Jayme and me financially, emotionally, and spiritually even before we knew of Neal's illness. We had enough money to stay in our home and enough that I didn't have to go to work. We had friends who supported us with invitations to their homes. We also had the opportunity to worship God in a new atmosphere.

A Second Chance at Happiness

As I dealt with widowhood, I finally began to know who I was and what I needed in order to feel secure. I was learning more about what being a Christian really meant. Since I had a young son to rear, I knew I wanted to remarry. Being married to a man of my faith was very important.

Seven months after Neal died I was reacquainted with my mother's friend, Betty. Betty did not know that my son Jayme was named after her son Jamie. Betty's husband, Jim, was so impressed with my Jayme's manners and personality that he asked if he could give his son my phone number. I agreed.

Soon after receiving my phone number, Jamie, Betty and Jim's son, called and we talked for more than an hour. We found there were many similarities in our lives, from each of us having been married to a person of the Jewish faith, to each having a little white dog. Jamie didn't know that my son was named after him, but once he found that out he wanted to meet his namesake. Jamie lived in Maryland, four hours away from my home in Pennsylvania. God had arranged our meeting by having Jamie's work send him to my area every other week. Jamie first came to dinner at my home in May of 1985.

As women often do, I fantasized that Jamie and I might connect and ultimately be married. Since I had known Jamie's family all my life, I felt comfortable in the idea that Jamie's faith was the same as mine and that we had a lot of things in common. Consequently, when Jamie told me that he had converted to Judaism while married to his first wife, I was shocked and dismayed. How could this be? I had known Jamie as a child, and I knew his parents. They were Christians. I truly didn't believe that Jamie could have turned away from Jesus, but God knew Jamie's heart.

Though Jamie and I had not seen each other for more than fifteen years, we had an immediate connection. Jamie started calling me every day. We dated and talked by phone throughout May and June. Then, on July 4, 1985, after dating only two months, Jamie asked me to marry him. I excitedly said yes. Our friends, family, and acquaintances were skeptical. However, we knew that it was the right thing to do.

A day or so after we became engaged, my cousin Barbara called me to say that the Lord had shown her that if Jamie and I were married before he accepted Jesus as his Savior, the marriage would not work. I accepted what Barbara said because I knew how difficult blending two religions had been during my previous marriage, and I didn't want that to happen again.

I called Jamie to tell him what Barbara had said. Jamie's reaction was, "Well, I guess we just can't get married." Although that was not what I wanted to hear, I knew that he was right. God had to come first in my life this time. After talking to Jamie, I called all my Christian girlfriends and asked them to start praying that Jamie would come to Christ.

Jamie agreed to read the Bible to learn about Jesus. He stayed up very late that night reading the book of Matthew. A few days later, on July 9th, Jamie came to my house. Before I could let him in the door, I needed to know what he had decided. He said that he had read the Bible and now believed that Jesus is the Messiah. Jamie was a Christian. I was ecstatic but my first words were "prove it." So Jamie took classes with my pastor and recommitted his life to Jesus on the same day that my son, Jayme, was baptized.

Jamie and I were married October 12, 1985 in a beautiful Christian ceremony. Young Jayme walked me down the aisle. My hands shook and my flowers quivered. Our wedding day was bright and sunny with the fall leaves of red, yellow, and brown all around. I was happy and secure again. This time I could be an authentic Christian woman living in a Christian community. I was secure in my belief in God since, even though I still bore pain from Neal's death, I had seen Him take me through widowhood into my new life.

Jayme and I moved to Maryland where Jamie lived. Young Jayme matured as big Jamie and I went to his basketball, football, and lacrosse games. Big Jamie truly became the father Neal had wished for us on our back deck when young Jayme asked what would happen after Neal died. I felt safe, secure, in love, and proud of both my husband and son.

Then one day the fear of what cancer could do to my life again reared its ugly head.

We had been married for almost fifteen years when Jamie began experiencing pain every time he swallowed. After a battery of tests, a CAT scan showed many cancerous spots throughout his body. Jamie had esophageal cancer that had metastasized to his liver and other areas of his body. There was no hope for a cure. Jamie went through chemotherapy because he was only forty-seven years old and wanted to prolong his life as much as possible. He died on my birthday, June 19, 2001, ten months after the diagnosis.

My pain associated with Neal's death was terrible, but since unresolved grief is cumulative, the pain associated with Jamie's death was many times greater.

Jamie and I were truly bonded. During those first months after Jamie died, I was surprised to see in a mirror that I was physically whole. I felt as though my midsection had been ripped out. I knew that I loved being a wife and could not understand why God would allow a wonderful marriage like ours to end so early. My only conclusion was that God had something for me to do that I couldn't do as Jamie's wife.

A *Tall, Blond Dance Partner*

Jamie's death caused me such great sadness that I couldn't even bear to listen to music. Music reminded me of happy times when I thought there would be no more sadness, and of times when I looked forward to the future. Now, music just made me hurt so badly that all I could do was cry. The rawness of my emotions lingered for many months. During that time I tried to exist without feeling anything because "feeling" equaled intense pain.

Knowing that I needed some way to meet new people and expand my world, I joined a Christian singles club. One time the club reserved a table at a place called Hollywood Ballroom. I was excited at the thought of dancing again, but I was apprehensive about hearing music. Would I cry rather than smile? After so many years of marriage, how would I react to dancing with men I didn't know? What would I wear? Would anyone ask me to dance? Could I still dance? Was this a safe place or would I be accosted by drunken men? I determined that I would never know the answers to those questions unless I took all the courage I had and went to the ballroom. What I didn't know was that my Lord had gone before me to prepare the way.

To my surprise, Hollywood Ballroom had a very large, beautiful wooden dance floor, not a postage-stamp-sized floor like so many places. The room had high ceilings, was smoke-free, and was filled with people who actually did ballroom dancing. There was a free lesson before the dance started where I was able to practice some of the steps I had learned as a girl. After that evening, I started going to the ballroom three times a week. Gradually my dancing improved to the point that during the lessons I was often selected to assist the instructor in demonstrating the new steps. I again felt special and my emotions associated with music moved from pain to enjoyment.

For a year and a half, I went to the ballroom by myself and came home by myself. Dancing was the activity that brought me back to life and began to ease my grief. Dancing allowed me to safely touch and be touched by another person. Ballroom dancing requires a strong "frame" where the woman's arms are stiff although bent. As I danced and talked with men, I gradually became more confident that I could return to the dating world and eventually, perhaps, have another man in my life. I danced because I loved to dance; I didn't dance because I wanted to meet my next husband. However, one tall, blond man was my favorite. I got to know him as we talked and laughed while we danced around and around the ballroom.

One night, after many months of dancing together, the handsome man asked if he could call me. From that time on, Glenn Kelly and I were together on and off the ballroom floor. A year later, we married.

Glenn and I have been happily married now for more than three years. We danced our way into marriage and are continuing to dance throughout our marriage. I have truly come from sorrow to dancing.

Chapter Two

The Losses We Face and the Questions We Ask

B ecoming a widow causes such a big change in your life that you may want to stay in bed all day with the covers over your head. You may feel a general sadness that seems to hang in the air like a heavy mist, never going away. You may even be angry that the world still turns on its axis when your world has collapsed around you. You may be angry with God for allowing your husband to die after all the prayer and other religious acts you and your friends performed.

"Why?"

WHY DID THIS HAVE TO HAPPEN? Your husband was a wonderful man who loved his family and did good things for others. Or perhaps your husband was not such a great father or husband, but you still loved him, so why did he have to die?

This question, and hundreds more, have been asked repeatedly by widows. Even when we think we know the answer, we probably don't. What good thing could come from such a tragedy? God says He has a plan for our lives which is for our good and not to harm us. How does the loss of a husband and father fit into such a plan?

I would encourage you to not only ask God your questions, but to journal them into a book where you can write all you are thinking and feeling. Write when you are happy, write when you are angry, and write when you are so sad the tears wet your paper.

Writing your thoughts will allow you to move the emotions and thoughts out of your head and onto paper. If you go back to read your journal later, you may see how you have progressed through your grief. You may also be reminded of issues that are still unresolved and need to be processed. Keeping the journal in a private place will allow you to write whatever you are thinking without worry that someone else will read it. You can express thoughts that you don't think are "proper" or that might be hurtful to someone else if they read the journal. If you like, destroy some of the pages after you write them . . . but please write them. Although you may never truly get an answer to "why," journaling will help you have more peace in your life.

"What Do I Do Now?"

Many widows ask "What do I do now?" All of the women I interviewed asked that question in one way or another. "What do I do now?" can mean so many things. For me, it meant "What is the next step? What do I have to do to get Neal's body out of the hospital? Is it my responsibility to call the funeral home? Do I accompany his body from the hospital to the funeral home?" For me, "What do I do now?" was a literal question.

For others, the words "What do I do now?" are more far-reaching and mean "What will my life be like?" or "What do I tell my children?" Asking "What do I do now?" is a valid question. Becoming a widow is a pivotal point in any woman's life. Her life will never be the same. She is no longer Mrs. John Doe. She has truly become Mary Doe. As Mary Doe, she will act in whatever way her personal crisis behavior dictates. She may shut down completely or become the comforter to others. She will probably go back to what she has known in the past until she moves from autopilot to a new life.

From the minute her husband dies, the choices a widow makes can affect the rest of her life. She can choose to be a victim or choose to overcome. She can choose to make good financial decisions or spend her money on frivolous things that dull her pain for the moment. She can choose to sell her house and start fresh somewhere new or stay where she is until she has allowed her mind to truly clear. Although the answer to "What do I do now?" is different in every circumstance, no matter what answer she receives to that question, the widow is ultimately responsible for what she does just as she was before she lost her spouse.

My Story with Neal

About three months after my first husband's diagnosis, I asked the oncologist where we were on the timeline of Neal's illness. I remember the doctor saying that Neal wasn't going to die the next day or next week, but that it would not be long. That statement has confirmed in my heart that doctors have no idea when someone will die because Neal died the next day.

As usual, on September 13, 1984, my telephone rang off the hook with calls from friends and family wanting to know the latest about Neal's condition. Due to these calls, I wasn't even able to take a shower and get ready for the day. My father had come from Pennsylvania to be with me and to help with my son. Jayme was at school, so Daddy and I planned to do a little shopping and then go to the hospital.

After taking several calls, I asked Daddy to answer the phone and to tell anyone who called that I could not talk. The phone rang again. This call was from Neal's former boss and good friend, Bill. Bill now lived many states away from us and was someone to whom I had not yet spoken, so I took his call. Bill and I talked for a long time. This call delayed my schedule long enough that I felt Daddy and I should rearrange our plans and go to the hospital before shopping.

Neal was in a hospital where I had been employed and had volunteered for several years. I knew many of the hospital staff. As Daddy and I walked through the lobby, I called a light and friendly "hello" to friends and acquaintances. I felt no sense of urgency to get to Neal's room until the elevator opened onto Neal's floor.

Having been tipped off by my friends who saw us cross the lobby, the hospital chaplain met us as we came off the elevator. He looked very concerned, but I didn't pick up on his intensity for a few moments. I smiled as I introduced the chaplain to my father. It never occurred to me that the chaplain was waiting at the elevator to intercept me before I got to Neal's room.

My mood changed as the chaplain said that something had happened and that the doctor wanted to talk with me. Daddy and I were taken to a small waiting area across from Neal's room where the doctor explained that Neal had died but they had been able to bring him back by using paddles and electronic shock to his heart. The doctor said Neal probably would not last very long and that I could go in to see him. All at once I felt very alone and frightened. I was afraid of what I would see when I entered Neal's room. I didn't know what to say to Neal. Would he hear me? What would comfort him? I had gone from my father's house to being Neal's wife and now my father was emotionally supporting me as I moved to the next stage of my life, being a widow at a time when I should have just been a soccer mom.

As I hurried across the hall, I asked Daddy to call my neighbor and ask her to pick up Jayme from school and bring him quickly to the hospital, to call my sister and ask her to start praying, and to ask Neal's sister to come as quickly as possible. The hospital had already called the rabbi. I went into Neal's room where I spent time telling him that everything would be all right. I asked him to hold on until Jayme got there. I assured Neal that Jayme was on his way.

In about a half hour, Jayme arrived with my friend. Within a short period, surrounded by people who loved him, Neal breathed his last breath. When he died, we were all quickly ushered out of Neal's room. Being a person who listens to authority, I left the room and went across the hall to the small waiting area where earlier I had met with the doctor.

I wanted to go back into Neal's room, so I got up and walked across the hall. The whole entourage followed me. They never allowed me to have time privately with Neal after he died. I regret not telling them that I wanted to be alone with Neal to say my good-bye. When we returned to the waiting room, I uttered the words almost all the women I interviewed ask, "What do I do now?"

Debby and Tom's Story

Debby came from a middle-class family. She always had the basic necessities but not too many frills. She went to college and later worked hard at her career. As a career woman, she had "enough" money but was far from rich. Then one day she met Tom. Tom was a bit older than Debby, and he was already established as a very successful entrepreneur. However, Tom was not good at taking care of himself.

Tom smoked, he had a lot of stress in his life, and he didn't exercise regularly. Debby described him as a "heart attack waiting to happen." One day, Tom woke Debby to say he thought he was having a heart attack. She called 911. Tom made it to the hospital but died shortly after arrival at the emergency room. Debby was instantly a young widow.

Although she had been living a very wealthy lifestyle while married to Tom, Debby had not been involved in the day-to-day financial decisions. She had a lot to learn and had to learn it very quickly. Debby's story may seem much better than those who are left with no funds, but she had even more to learn than her sister widows. Having an extremely large amount of money is a great responsibility.

Debby's ability to handle problems and crises came in handy. She began doing what she knew needed to be done to carry on with the business. She also helped other family members get through the shock of Tom's sudden death. However, she did not allow herself to feel the pain of Tom's death for years.

Debby was angry at Tom for not taking care of his health, and she wanted to be alone with her anger. She did not want to be consoled. Her dreams of retirement with Tom and having him all to herself were gone in an instant due to his unhealthy habits. A long time passed before the impact of what had happened hit Debby. She made decisions but didn't allow herself to feel. For weeks after Tom's death, she wanted to yell and scream, but it was not in her nature to show emotion around others so she ignored her emotions. She was operating like a robot. It was seven years before she could clearly think about the events of Tom's death and analyze them rationally.

Debby asked "What do I do now?" immediately after Tom's death and again months later as she realized the magnitude of her fortune and her grief. In order to maintain her sanity and have a reason to get up each day, Debby initially filled her days with volunteer work. Today she continues to volunteer much of her time. She runs several large charities. She has not remarried. Although being single is sometimes socially uncomfortable, she feels she is secure and complete in her life. Debby is fun to be around and inspires others to move through difficulties in life. She certainly does not embody my former stereotype of widowhood.

Flo's Story

Flo has been widowed twice. She was a teenager when she married her first husband, Joe. Joe was also a teenager. They were married for several years, but he was in the service and stationed away from home for much of their marriage. One night Flo dreamed that a military man came to her home to notify her of Joe's death. Two days later, the military chaplain came with another officer and made her worst nightmare come true. Her young husband had been killed in Vietnam.

Joe had been away for much of their marriage. After his death, life seemed very much the same as before. Flo just kept doing what she had been doing. With no income, no college degree, and no career, Flo had to find a job to support herself and her three children. She never grieved Joe's passing. Flo was in her mid-twenties when she first became a widow.

Eventually Flo met Hal. They dated for four years then blended their two families through marriage. They added their own child to the mix and raised six children. After almost twenty wonderful years of marriage, Flo and Hal were finally empty nesters in their early fifties. They bought land in a southern state and were making plans to build their retirement home when Hal was diagnosed with terminal cancer. He was treated with chemotherapy and radiation. He lived another five years before the cancer took his life.

Flo asked "What do I do now?" twice. The first time, she knew the answer was that she had to keep going for her children. However, when her second husband, Hal, died, she was truly alone for the first time in her life. "What do I do now?" was a plaintive cry to God to help her emotionally heal from her great losses. All her dreams were gone. Again, Flo threw herself into her work, eventually met another man, and remarried. Flo thought working at her job was the way to move through the grief.

Although Flo kept busy with work and children, she too ignored the pain that needed to be grieved. Several years after Hal died, Flo initiated a grief group at her church. She works with other widows and has finally begun to grieve for both of her deceased husbands.

Linda and Carl's Story

Linda was widowed at thirty-three with two small sons, ages three and five. She and Carl had moved to Virginia just six months prior to the time when a simple visit to his father turned deadly for Carl.

Carl and his father were on a three-day weekend vacation at the Grand Canyon when Carl decided to go hiking alone. Linda had not expected to talk with Carl from the time he left on Friday until he returned home on Sunday, so when the phone rang in the middle of the night Saturday night, she was alarmed. On the phone was Linda's father-in-law saying that Carl was missing. Linda, a devout Christian, prayed over the telephone with her father-in-law for Carl's safe return. She assured her father-in-law that everything would be fine. Then Linda waited about an hour before calling one of her friends for support. The friend started crying and feared the worst, so Linda comforted her friend. Instead of being comforted by others, Linda was playing the role of the comforter.

Early the next morning, Linda called other friends, and some of them came to spend the day with her. Every few hours the police from Nevada called to say that they still knew nothing. They asked upsetting questions such as, "Does Carl know how to handle himself in open spaces?"

Friends called and cried but Linda did not cry. She felt sure God was with Carl and that he would be rescued. During the crisis, Linda was on autopilot. She took care of her sons and consoled others as she waited for word of Carl's safe return.

On Sunday evening at seven o'clock, the Nevada coroner called to say Carl's body had been recovered from the bottom of the Grand Canyon. His body was in the coroner's office. Linda realized that even though God was with Carl, Carl was dead.

She asked, "What do I do now?" Sadly, Linda's next steps included flying to Nevada to claim her husband's body and having him buried in Texas.

The Answer to "What do I do now?" may be "Grieve."

You may feel completely in control of your life, your emotions, and all the things you do. However, every widow with whom I spoke admitted that she had been in shock and in a fog immediately following her husband's death. Some women admitted that it took many months or even several years to come out of the fog. Unfortunately, none realized she was in a fog until she had emerged from it. Perhaps that is why the common recommendation is that a widow should delay making important decisions for at least a year.

When Neal died, I didn't want to turn into the stereotype of the unhappy woman with black clothes and a harsh attitude that I had pictured from my childhood. I was thirty-five years of age with a young son. I knew I had to do whatever it took to rear my boy into manhood, but I had no clue how to do that. As I had done throughout my life, I relied on those around me to lead me. My father, my stepfather, my sister, and others all had opinions about what I should do. I was willing to listen and ultimately, I usually made the right decision because I took things slowly and tried to consider the consequences of each decision before it was made.

As you walk through the days shortly after your husband's death, please delay as many big decisions as possible. The time will come when your thoughts will be clear again and when you can make those decisions rationally. Rely only on people who have your best interest at heart. Although women often have a hard time accepting help, please know that you are the one who now needs help. You will have many opportunities to be helpful to others in the future. So, what do you do now? Grieve.

Chapter Two
Discussion Questions

1. Did you ask the question "What do I do now?"?

2. How have you answered that question?

3. As you grieve your husband's death are you also grieving other losses? Please journal about all the losses in your life and how those losses have affected you.

Chapter Three

Things People Say

When I was a child my mother often quoted the saying "Sticks and stones may break your bones but words can never hurt you." I used to quote it myself until I realized how untrue it is. I have been hurt by words more than sticks and stones, and I know that my words have sometimes been hurtful. When someone is ill or dies, people feel the need to offer comfort, but what they say can sometimes make the situation worse. Other times, one special person's words can make all the difference.

Words that Hurt

Each time I became a widow I was told how "strong" I was. Although those who said I was strong were probably trying to comfort me, what I heard was, "You are strong and can handle losing one or two husbands but I am weak and would crumble under that stress so God would never let that happen to me (I hope)." In other words, I heard them trying to reassure themselves that they didn't fit the mold to be a widow and therefore should be spared the pain. I remember being so angry when I was told I was strong that I wanted to yell, "Yeah, well I'm not any stronger than you are and yes, you might be widowed too some day!" What made God look down and point me out as "strong"? Why should I have to start over twice and lose my husbands and the fathers of my child? Was that fair?

One of my most painful experiences was when I went to a new doctor for a checkup shortly after Jamie died. While telling my history, I mentioned that I had been widowed twice. This unthinking man said, "Boy, I bet no one else will want to date you."

I was shocked at his insensitivity and burst into tears. His words had exposed my deepest fear and I cried almost uncontrollably for several minutes. Needless to say, he realized his error immediately and started apologizing.

I finally composed myself and went through with the examination. When I reached my home after the appointment there were beautiful flowers on my doorstep with a note of sincere apology from the doctor. Although I never returned to that doctor, I give him credit for realizing his insensitivity and for apologizing.

Over time, I have healed and mellowed. As I have moved through the grief and pain, I realize that people simply don't know what to say. I must give them the grace to say the wrong thing.

Words that Heal

Although some people said the wrong thing to me, there was one special woman who forever changed my outlook. Her name is Pam. Pam and I had been neighbors when Jayme, my son, was a toddler. After moving away from the neighborhood where Pam lived, I lost touch with her. Twenty years passed. Neal had died, Jayme had become a young man, and I had remarried when I saw Pam again. We reconnected a couple of times but as I was busy trying to do everything possible to save Jamie's life, Pam and I lost touch again.

When I reconnected with Pam and told her that I had been widowed for the second time, I was slightly embarrassed. Being widowed once is bad enough, but twice . . . well, how do you explain it? The response I received from

Pam was one of the pivotal times in my life. Pam's comment was that God had honored me by allowing me to take two men to the ends of their lives. What a different perspective Pam had on my life!

As I thought about Pam's words, I remembered that God has a plan for my life and that plan may not always be fun. The idea that God would think enough of me to allow me to do all the things associated with nursing two husbands through cancer allowed me to realize I have a purpose, and that God hasn't forgotten me. I am forever grateful to Pam for changing the way I look at my life.

Jean and Greg's Story

Jean and Greg had a stormy marriage. He had been previously married and was a widower. Jean had never been married before she married Greg. Greg suffered from a mental disorder which made living with him very difficult. He was up one day and down the next. They tried very hard to stay together but after several years, Jean had had enough and she separated from Greg. It was during that time of separation that Greg's depression became extreme and he committed suicide.

Because they were separated and Greg was living alone at the time of his death, Jean didn't know anything was wrong for several days. Greg was found by his adult son who notified Jean that Greg was dead. Jean felt guilty that she hadn't found Greg and that she hadn't known he was so depressed that he could harm himself. Throughout the time Jean had known Greg there had been threats of suicide, but Greg had never actually done anything to hurt himself. In her grief, shock, and pain, Jean reached out to friends and family. The responses she received were worse than she ever expected.

Some family members questioned Jean's sorrow since she and Greg were not living together at the time of his death. The worst part was that some individuals actually blamed Jean for Greg's death. Whether or not Greg and Jean were happily married, she was not responsible for his decisions. It took Jean several years of counseling and prayer to undo the harm done by those who should have been comforting her but who, in their own pain, needed a scapegoat. Although she has forgiven them, Jean will probably never completely forget the additional pain she felt due to their unkind words.

Instead of calling to console Jean when the word of Greg's death got out, friends and acquaintances started calling to offer advice. Within days of Greg's death, one acquaintance offered the name of a realtor who could help Jean sell her house and someone else offered to assist Jean at starting a home-based business. Although these individuals thought they were being helpful, they may have been acting out of their own needs more than Jean's need.

Jean told the story of how her friends gathered around her immediately after her husband's death but they didn't allow her to determine the course of the conversation. They talked incessantly about subjects other than the tragedy. They tried to distract her when she needed to embrace the shock of knowing that Greg had committed suicide. She was experiencing guilt, shame, anger, remorse, sadness, and shock. When her friends talked about inconsequential topics, she wanted to tell them to go away.

Linda's Forgiveness

After Carl's accidental death at the Grand Canyon, Linda had to deal with pity. People said things like, "You poor thing, this must be so awful." She was insulted by their pity because she knew God had a plan. Carl's death was part of the plan. People also began to tell Linda how to live and act. Linda now recognizes that their unsolicited advice was driven by their own fears and had nothing to do with her situation. She had to hold her tongue in order not to lash out at their insensitivity. The things people say are almost always meant to heal but often they add to the widow's pain and anger.

Your Choice

The world is filled with words. Most people are trying to help even when their words are not seen as helpful. Just as I had to forgive those who hurt me, you may have to forgive someone. As in all things, we cannot control what someone says to or about us, but we can choose how we receive what is said.

If you find yourself feeling hurt or angry after speaking with someone, think about what was said. Did the unthinking person say something hurtful on purpose, or out of his or her own fear? Whether or not it was said to hurt you, forgiveness can only come from you. Lack of forgiveness breeds bitterness. Bitterness hurts only the one who holds it, not the one at whom it is aimed.

I urge you not to allow words or circumstances to make you bitter. The bitter person doesn't often realize she is seen that way. How can you know if you have become bitter? Observe how you feel. Are you angry and uptight when you hear about good things happening to others? Do you lack peace and serenity? Do you feel the need to get revenge? These are all signs of bitterness.

The antidote to bitterness is forgiveness. Forgiveness doesn't require that you contact the people who have made you angry to tell them they are forgiven. It also doesn't require that the people who hurt you apologize. In fact, they may not even be aware that they have hurt you.

Forgiveness requires that you try to understand the other person's motives. The way you feel about life will change as you begin to appreciate the good things you experience. Are you feeling less stress and anger? Are you less fearful? These feelings are all part of the serenity which accompanies having a forgiving spirit. They are the signs that joy is returning to your life.

Chapter Three
Discussion Questions

1. What has been said that added pain or anger to your life? What have you done with those feelings?

2. What has been said that added joy or redefinition of your pain?

3. Have you forgiven those who hurt you?

Chapter Four

That's What Friends Are For

My Friends at Neal's Death

When you are hurting, there is no better person in the world than a friend. Two women stand out in my memory for the special treatment they provided around the time of Neal's death. Donna, the wife of a local doctor and a busy socialite whom I had only known from afar, started calling me daily when she heard that Neal was sick. She didn't call to gossip or make small talk; she called to see if I needed help. Although Donna didn't really live close to our house, she would let me know where her daily travels were taking her to see if I needed anything from the grocery store or the drug store. I was initially hesitant to allow her to do anything for me until I realized that she truly enjoyed having the opportunity of making my life easier.

When Neal died, Donna wanted to stay at my house during the funeral because she had heard that houses were sometimes robbed when the family was at a funeral. When we returned from the cemetery, Donna had prepared a sumptuous dinner for all of my friends and family. More than twenty-three years later, I still feel tremendous love and gratitude for Donna. I have not seen her in all these years, but I will never forget her kindness.

Shortly after Neal died, another lady, whom I will call Victoria, asked what she could do for me. I couldn't think of anything. I requested that she call me in three months when

I felt most of the others would have gone back to their lives. Believe it or not, she called three months later. What a kind, kind gesture. I still didn't need anything, but just the thought that she remembered to call me has kept her in my memory all these years.

Neal's illness and death caused my closest friends to rally around me in a very protective fashion. All of sudden, my son and I were being invited to dinner at friends' homes during the week and for special holiday dinners. I usually accepted these invitations because I felt that if these people were willing to welcome us into their homes, we should be willing to enjoy their hospitality.

These social encounters were important for several reasons. First, it showed my nine-year-old son that our lives had not ended. People still liked Jayme and me and wanted to have us around. It was okay to laugh, play, and joke even though we were in pain. Second, I think we helped those people we visited to see that there is life after the death of a loved one. I hope we set a good example and honored my deceased husband's memory as we moved on in our lives.

My Friends after Jamie's Death

A few days after my second husband, Jamie, died, I got a call from a longtime friend named Judi. Judi said that she would like to visit me. I thought she would come for the afternoon. However, when Judi got out of her car, she began pulling out luggage. She said she would stay as long as I needed her.

Boy, did I need her. Judi has always been a godsend to anyone who needs a listening ear, a shoulder to cry on, and true love from a friend. Judi came in, sat down, and listened to whatever I wanted to say. She asked if there were any things with which I needed her help. We pulled down the canopy from my bed and ran it through the dryer to get the dust out, she helped me decipher how to tape programs on the VCR, and we talked.

Judi only offered advice when asked and then the advice was offered in such a loving manner that even in such a wounded state, I couldn't be offended. We went to dinner at a restaurant Jamie and I had loved because I knew it would be terribly hard to go to that restaurant without him. Doing anything for the first time without the most important person in your life can be devastating, but doing it with a friend who will allow you to reminisce and cry if you need to makes the task a little easier.

Although I was not afraid to stay alone in my home, having Judi in the house was comforting. Just having someone say "good night" helped. After a few days, I felt I could handle being alone, so Judi went home. I knew that Judi would come back if I needed her.

As the months moved on, sometimes I just needed to get out of my house for a while. That is when I would call Lucy. Lucy allowed me to hang out at her house. She was never too busy to have me drop by. I tried not to overstay my welcome. I enjoyed being at her house, having coffee, and talking, talking, talking.

Both Lucy and Judi had been my friends for several years when Jamie died, so I didn't have to explain what I had been through. They had walked with me through the good times and the pain of Jamie's illness and death. My longtime friends were invaluable. However, new friends helped me to move through the grief as well.

New friends can come from anywhere. The members of my grief group became very special friends. Seven people who would probably never have been friends under other circumstances attended the twelve-week hospice grief course. Our group included a diplomat, two female corporate vice presidents, a man who had retired from the U.S. government, an arborist, a lady who had a house cleaning business, and me. Our ages ranged from early forties to the seventies. Our religions were all different. All had children. Some had grown children; others had children who still lived at home. We became great friends and were able to share intimate details of our experiences because we had one thing in common: we had all lost our spouses. Although most groups disband when the formal course is finished, after our twelve-week course ended, our group met together monthly at one of our homes. We still needed each other.

This group filled a void in each of our lives. We cared about each other and bonded until one by one, we began to move from our grief to our new lives. Although we each mourned the loss of the new friends as the group began to break up, we knew that we had come together for a purpose and that purpose had been fulfilled.

Some people shun the widow to protect themselves from "catching" the terrible ailment of widowhood. What they may be expressing is their fear of losing a loved one. They cannot imagine how they would live through such a tragedy, and rather than try to get outside of their own fears to comfort the widow, they move away from her as fast as possible.

If you encounter this treatment from strangers you might just ignore it, conduct the business you have to conduct with them, and move on. However, if your closest friend begins to shun you because of her fears, you may need to talk with her about it. After my second husband died of cancer, one of my female co-workers began asking me to go to dinner every so often. We had lovely chats about what was going on in her life and in mine. She listened as I reminisced about my deceased husband and we grew to be good friends. Then I stopped hearing from her. When she finally answered one of my phone messages, she said that her husband was undergoing treatment for cancer.

Although we talked about what she was going through and I tried to be as supportive to her as she had been to me, our relationship had changed. She had been friendly when I needed support, but she was unable to receive support when her husband was ill. Although I was saddened by this turn of events, I let her know that I was available to support her if she wanted me.

A major life change affects all areas of one's life. You may lose some friends in the process but you will probably gain others. You are not responsible for how other people act. You must accept them for who they are as you move forward with or without them. The list of our friends changes during our lives whether we encounter tragedies or not. Please look at a loss of friendships as a forced growth experience and appreciate the friends who remain.

Chapter Four
Discussion Questions

1. Do you have friends who have helped you get through the grieving process?

2. What contribution has each friend made?

3. Has your relationship changed with any longtime friends? Is that change good or bad?

Chapter Five

Grieving: A Stage or Destination

Holding On

Becoming a widow happens in an instant. Moving away from widowhood takes much longer and requires moving away from the memory of the husband you loved. It is one of the hardest things you will ever do. It is also one of the last tasks of grieving. This radical idea may make you angry. You may think that I am wrong and that it doesn't apply to you. You could be right. You may choose not to move away from your husband's memory, but if you make that choice, you may be choosing to remain stuck in widowhood.

Moving away from Jamie's memory began as I attended a grief group. When my first husband, Neal, died I didn't feel I wanted to sit around and hear about other people's sadness. I went to one grief group meeting and decided it wasn't for me. Consequently, I probably didn't grieve Neal's death fully until many years later. Although not everyone wants to go to a formal grief group, I would highly recommend that you try it for a few sessions before you decide whether or not it will help. Hospice and religious organizations employ individuals who know how to facilitate a group to make sure everyone gets a chance to talk and that all needs are met. Although you can go through the grieving process with a friend, the burden of all your sorrow will fall on the friend.

That burden may be very great. I recommend talking with friends while attending a grief group for the formal support.

After Jamie died I thought I didn't need a grief group. I had been through widowhood before. I felt sure I knew how to handle grief. However, I was wrong.

Jamie and I attended a church where he was an official and where we were very active. Our friends from church kept in close contact with us during Jamie's illness. He was on the prayer list for months and was even asked to tell his story at the Easter service when he was undergoing chemotherapy. After he died, I knew going to church would be difficult, but I never imagined how difficult it could be.

One Sunday morning, a few weeks after Jamie died, I went to church alone. It was a beautiful morning. I greeted friends and took a seat in the back, away from where Jamie and I usually sat. The familiar music started and I began to feel emotional. I stayed as long as I could, but in about five minutes I knew I was going to be unable to contain my tears. I left the service. Once in my car, I cried and cried as I drove home. I thought my heart would break and that I would be unable to breathe. Through my tears, I somehow made it home where I immediately called my next-door-neighbor, Kerry.

When Kerry heard my voice, she knew something was wrong. I asked if she could come over right away. She was at my door in about two minutes. As I opened the door, she could see that I was crying hysterically. Through my sobs, I tried to explain that I just didn't know how I would make it this time. Kerry quietly sat with me as I sobbed for almost thirty minutes. Finally, I calmed down enough that she felt she could leave me alone. Kerry's presence helped me get through that terrible bout of grieving. Although she wasn't sure what to do for me, she sat beside me and allowed me to do what I had to do—cry. The next day I called hospice to ask about joining a grief group where I could learn to deal with my pain.

The first group I attended was what they called a "drop in" group. It was informal with no structure to the session. Sometimes there were as many as ten widows and widowers in attendance, but many times there were only three of us.

The sessions were held in a classroom of a church. A social worker ran the sessions to make sure no one monopolized the time. The social worker asked questions and usually had a general topic to start the conversation. I found the informality of this group to be helpful because I could talk about whatever was on my mind that week. We discussed preparations for the first holidays without our spouses, grocery shopping, and many other subjects.

After about four months of attending this group, I decided that I was ready for a more structured setting where I would be expected to follow their plan and do homework. The course was twelve weeks long and included men and women. Again, we met once a week.

During the first session we were asked to write our goals concerning grieving for our spouses. The goal sheets were collected by the social worker with the promise that they would be returned to us at the end of the course. My goals included my desire to end the yearning to see Jamie again. Throughout the class, each member was given an opportunity to tell the story of how his or her spouse died. We heard about each one's children, job, as well as dashed hopes and dreams. We cried for each other and began to bond.

The final session was bittersweet. We knew we had come a long way together during those twelve weekly sessions. At the last session our instructor had a special ceremony for us. During the ceremony, we each talked about our deceased spouse and showed a piece of memorabilia from our marriages. Then we each read our goal sheets from the first class aloud and lit a candle to signify reaching the goal.

During the class discussions about moving through grief, the instructor had told us that we would have to move away from the memory of our former lives. Until I lit the candle, I didn't know if I would be able to move away from Jamie's memory. My piece of memorabilia was a video tape of the talk Jamie had given to our church on Easter Sunday, two months before he died. In the video, Jamie recounted the story of how he and I met and how he accepted Jesus as his Savior. Jamie told the congregation that although he was fighting esophageal cancer, he had hope because of his faith. His hope was in Jesus. Jamie knew he would go to heaven when he died.

As I lit the candle after showing the video, I knew that I would be able to move a little further away from Jamie's memory. Jamie had moved on and so should I.

Cry

Cry to relieve the stress. Some days you may feel so exhausted that you don't see how you can go on, and yet you cry. Crying truly helps relieve stress and provides comfort. Slowly, over time, crying happens less and less. One way to know that you are getting stronger and moving through grief is by how often, how long, and how intensely you cry.

Debby's Way of Coping

When Debby's husband, Tom, died suddenly of a heart attack, she was emotionally unprepared for the loss. Instead of going to a grief group, Debby got busy with a project at her church helping remodel the church kitchen. This project allowed her to direct her energy in a positive way as she went to meetings, made new friends, and used her corporate experience to enhance the church. However, Debby did not grieve. She was simply distracted. *Distraction and denial do not equal grieving.* It took Debby almost seven years to move through her grief. Could she have reached the same emotional stability in less time if she had worked with a counselor or grief group? We will never know. Each person makes the choice to move through grief in her own way, at her own pace. Even if Debby could have moved through more quickly, she might have chosen the slower pace because moving through grief means moving away from the lost loved one.

A Stage or Destination

We go through many stages in life. We are infants, toddlers, children, teenagers, and adults. Even being an adult includes stages such as young adult, thirty-something, midlife, senior, and elderly adults. As we go through the stages determined by our ages, we also go through other stages. Life and time continue to move forward whether we move with them or not. We must make choices all day long, every day. The idea of not making a choice is actually making a choice. The final destination of life is death. On the way to our final destination, we can make positive decisions to impact others with joy and leave sunshine in our tracks, or we can impact them with our pain and leave unsightly tracks.

When we do not confront the pain associated with our losses, it is stored somewhere in our bodies. Like a blemish, the pain will remain under the skin for a very long time waiting for the right pressure to make it explode. Because it is ugly, those with whom we come in contact will try to look anywhere except at that blemish. Looking at an ugly blemish almost makes it seem to grow. No one wants to be around when the infection is released from its thin covering of skin. However, until the release happens, covering the blemish with makeup only works for a little while; pretending it isn't there doesn't remove it. Everyone knows it is unsightly and painful. Only the person in whose body the blemish resides can take the steps that make it go away. Confronting pain, just like lancing a blemish, cleanses the body of infection.

All of my good times and hard times have been integrated to make me who I am. The same thing is true of each of us. We are made up of the myriad of things we have done and things which have been done to us. Again, we choose how we view these things. We are victims or we are overcomers. I chose to overcome. If you want, you can too.

Chapter Five
Discussion Questions

1. Do you cry? What prompts you to cry?

2. How do you handle crying?

3. Do you cry alone or are there people who will support you as you cry?

4. How do you feel about the loss of your husband? Please describe the emotions you are experiencing and how you handle them.

5. Have you begun to think about moving away from your husband?

6. Have you decided to make grief a stage or a destination in your life?

Chapter Six

Taking Care of Yourself

Moving away from Jamie was one of the hardest, yet most necessary things for me to do in order to move toward the rest of my life. I had to confront my pain by feeling it, talking about it, and realizing that the pain should not rule my life. I felt that God's plan for me did not include wallowing in this pain forever. I had to choose whether or not I would continue walking the path God had for me or move away from God because I didn't like where His plan had taken me. My choice was to continue down God's path in the presence of my Lord Jesus because He was my husband now that Jamie was gone.

Groceries and Cooking

Unexpected emotion can come up at the grocery store, while riding in the car, or at any place where you and your husband spent time together. Grocery shopping is often hard because over time, throughout our marriages, we change our eating habits to accommodate our husbands' likes and dislikes.

When we begin buying for ourselves alone, we may reach for items that we bought for our husbands and wonder if the item is really one that WE like or if we are still buying for him. Although this realization shows movement through grief, in the beginning it is an extremely painful realization. Again we are confronted with the aloneness of being a widow.

I remember walking through the grocery store as quickly as I could because the background music made me remember feelings from prior times when I was a homemaker buying things my husband and son liked to eat. My second husband, Jamie, liked a certain type of applesauce. When we married, I started buying his brand and stopped buying the brand I had previously bought. After he died, I still bought Jamie's favorite applesauce. One day, as I reached for it, I remembered that I had bought a different brand before Jamie came into my life. However, I decided that I had grown to enjoy Jamie's favorite so I would continue to buy that one. This simple decision brought pain because I remembered the feelings associated with buying Jamie's favorite as a gift to him. I had felt the joy of nurturing my husband by doing something as simple as changing to his brand of applesauce. Then I remembered that he wasn't going to eat it or enjoy it when I brought it home. Buying that brand now had to be because I liked it, not because he did. Only another widow would understand that deciding which brand of applesauce to buy would be a major decision that could bring pain.

Cooking, another nurturing activity, became so difficult for me that I completely stopped cooking. I blocked out the memory of what I ate day to day because food brought back painful memories. I existed on TV dinners and Harvard-style red beets. Sadness is stronger when we are tired or hungry. Even if you don't want to cook, you must eat. When Jamie died, I felt that I needed to reduce my pain so I ate ice cream. I do not recommend eating a large dish of ice cream every evening as I did. You can guess what happened; I put on weight. One day a friend mentioned my weight. Even though I was insulted, I began to realize that I had to stop eating so many sweets. After all, the ice cream did not reduce my pain, and I began to hate the way I looked. Now I had two problems! When I stopped eating the ice cream and started dancing, I released fifteen pounds without even dieting. A few little changes can make all the difference.

Exercise

I encourage you to exercise regularly even if you have never exercised before! Exercise releases endorphins in the brain that are natural painkillers. People who exercise often begin to feel better because of the endorphins and because they are taking charge of their lives. They are not victims of their circumstances. The added benefit of looking better will help as you see yourself in the mirror every day and begin to realize that you are still alive and life is worth living.

Share Your Story

Let others know what has happened to you. Sharing your story will help it become real in your mind. The more you tell your story, the less you will cry when you tell it, and the more control you will have over your emotions. The terrible loss really happened to you but it does not have to destroy you. You must make the choice of how you respond to life every minute of every day.

Keep in touch with friends and family—please don't isolate yourself from others. Although you do need time alone to cry, yell, journal your feelings, think about what has happened, deal with financial issues, and just sleep, you can be alone too much.

Keep busy enough that the days don't drag on and on, but don't be too busy to grieve. Grieving takes time. It doesn't happen in a sequential manner where you can say, "I am so glad I am through that part of the grieving cycle." You may go through one part and then come back to that same part months later. I am not sure that humans ever completely finish grieving someone they love.

Beverly and Mark's Story

Beverly and Mark were married for many years. Mark was a fitness buff who exercised and took very good care of himself. Beverly hated exercise and was a bit overweight. Beverly and Mark loved to laugh. They often joked that Beverly would die first and Mark would have her ashes on the mantle where she could watch to be sure he didn't take up with a floozy. Mark would reply that people would just put their cigarettes out in Beverly's ashes, and he would again remind her that she was gaining weight.

They talked about each one's desires after death such as funeral preferences, cremation or burial, where to keep the ashes after cremation, and so on. But they never got around to filling out living wills or sharing day-to-day financial information.

During an otherwise uneventful period in their lives, Mark had an upset stomach that his doctor attributed to the flu. Since Mark didn't appear to be getting better, the doctor ran blood tests. While Beverly and Mark were waiting for the blood test results, Mark experienced a strange episode at work. He was working on a report when all of a sudden nothing made sense. He even had trouble turning off his computer and got lost on the way home from work. Mark had had a small stroke.

A few days after the stroke, the blood tests came back and showed that Mark was suffering from pancreatic cancer. In less than a week, Beverly and Mark had gone from being a happy, empty-nest couple to a couple fighting cancer and the results of a stroke. The doctor was pessimistic about the ability to cure Mark's cancer and recommended that Mark simply enjoy the few months he had left. After about three months, Mark had another stroke then died a week later.

Mark's first stroke left him unable to read or write but he insisted on continuing to pay the household bills. Although

Beverly was very well educated and had a high-level government job, she didn't know about the family finances. Mark asked Beverly to learn about their finances many times over their long marriage but she refused. After Mark's death, Beverly had a very hard time determining what needed to be paid and where the bank accounts were kept.

While still grieving, Beverly had to learn about finances, taxes, daily bills, where Mark kept checkbooks, as well as what bills needed to be paid. She thought she would never climb out from under the weight of this new responsibility. Plus, she found that during his three-month illness, Mark had neglected to pay some very important bills. Beverly's anger at Mark for leaving her in such a mess helped her to move through her grief.

Beverly worked with a grief coach after Mark's death. The coach encouraged Beverly to do what she could as quickly as she could but didn't push her too fast. Beverly found that if she just couldn't bear to work on the financial mess one day, she could do it the next day. Eventually Beverly went back to her government job and life became routine. She was moving through the grief to the next stage of her life. She began to enjoy simple pleasures like going to the vacation home she had shared with Mark. Beverly may never remarry, but she has her job and enjoys her life. She has learned how to take care of her finances and how to care for her other needs.

Lori and Frank's Story

Lori and Frank were married for more than thirty years. Frank was the master in the family. He wanted everything his way and was difficult to live with. His children and wife loved him in spite of how mean he treated them. Frank controlled everything in the family's lives. Nothing Lori did was good enough for Frank. After doing his laundry, she was not allowed to put it away but had to stack it on Frank's side of the bed for Frank to place it in his chest of drawers the way he wanted it. Lori was not even allowed to move Frank's shoes from where he put them under the bed.

One day Frank began to notice a pain in his leg. His doctor said it was arthritis, a result of having had Lyme's Disease. Before long, Frank began to have black and blue marks all over his body except in his legs. The doctor prescribed an x-ray, MRI, and bone scan. The diagnosis was then changed from arthritis to bone cancer which had metastasized to the blood, brain, and all over Frank's body. The doctor said the leg pain was referred pain from the other areas. Frank immediately started radiation therapy.

Initially, Frank refused to allow Lori to tell the family what was happening. However, after the third week of treatment, because of the terminal diagnosis, the doctor recommended that Frank tell his mother and children about his illness.

A few weeks later, in severe pain, Frank could no longer walk up the stairs at their home and he began saying strange things. Frank was admitted to the hospital. In his delirium, Frank didn't want to stay in the hospital because he was sure there were terrorists in the hospital who wanted to kill him.

Eventually, Frank's mean nature began to show itself not only to his family but to the hospital staff as well. He ranted and raved at the top of his lungs. By this time, against the stipulations of his living will, Frank had been connected to many machines. The doctor told Lori that Frank would die in two days. Although Lori and her daughters were angry at the doctor for what they thought was a callous discussion of when their husband and father would die, the doctor was right. Two days after being removed from the machines, Frank died. The irony of Frank's death was that only after Frank had died, was Lori able to start living again.

Although she had lived in the same house more than thirty years, after Frank died Lori began to worry about being alone in the house and what would happen to her if she got sick or needed full-time care. Although she didn't realize it at the time, Lori began to move through her grief when she had a security system installed and when she purchased long-term care insurance. She immediately felt secure in her house and she knew that with the long-term care insurance she would not have to rely on her children to take care of her. She could remain independent.

Frank's need to control extended past his death. He put notes all around the house for Lori before he went into the hospital. The notes told her what to do and how to live even after he was gone. Lori was so dominated by Frank's presence that even after he died she was unable to put his clean clothes into a drawer, let alone give them away. For months after Frank died, the clothing stayed on his side of the bed since he was not there to put them away.

Setting a goal to become your own person is important in taking care of yourself. Lori's husband had been extremely harsh and domineering. When he died, Lori had to decide how to deal with life when no one was telling her every move to make. She attended a grief group for a while and then decided that individual therapy might be helpful. Therapy helped Lori gain the courage to move forward in her life. I watched her move from a cowering widow who dressed only in black for the first year after her husband died, to a confident mother and grandmother who enjoys swimming, crafts, going out with friends, and remodeling her home!

Flo's Way of Coping

Taking care of yourself as you find your place in society can also be difficult. Flo, widowed twice, reported that she did not grieve her first husband's death. When her first husband died, she had been busy with her children. After her second husband's death, she was busy with her job and still did not go to grief groups or do any formal grieving. She simply didn't know how to grieve. To move on with her life, Flo tried to get involved with activities at her church but nothing worked. She did not fit in with the couples and divorced singles.

About two years after her second husband died, Flo was still grieving and unable to move forward in life. She went to a women's conference and found out about a grief group that she could start in her church. By starting the group for others, Flo learned to grieve. Flo has retired from her career and now gives her time to help other widows walk through their grief. She admits that helping others was what ultimately helped her, and she continues to grieve as she works with new widows.

Pain

Feeling the pain of loss is almost the only way to allow the pain to heal and go away. If you deny the pain, it will hide inside you. It will come out at the most unexpected time and you may not even recognize it for what it is. I have felt physical pain in my abdomen with the loss of each of my husbands. The pain was so intense that it doubled me over. The things that seemed to relieve the pain were crying, talking about my feelings, and prayer.

The amount of preparation we have for our spouse's death helps determine how quickly we move through the pain. Widows whose husbands die of heart attacks or in accidents have no preparation. They have to deal with the trauma of the sudden change while grieving the loss. I have met widows who, at the second or third anniversary of their husbands' deaths, still seemed unprepared to go on living. Each situation is different. Wherever you are in the process, please know that it is okay. Your grief timeline is up to you, no one else.

Chapter Six
Discussion Questions

1. How are you meeting your physical, mental, and spiritual needs?

2. Do you identify with any of the women's stories given above?

Chapter Seven

Special Times with God

Where is God while you are crying and when you feel like you cannot go on? He is right where He has always been in your life. If you know God and walk with Him daily, you will probably continue to walk with Him. If you don't know God, your pain may be what brings you to Him.

I know God through Jesus Christ. It is because of this knowledge that I was able to move through my times of grief. Yes, I asked God "Why?" No, He didn't answer me directly, but He did answer with His Word.

> Peter, an apostle of Jesus Christ,
> To God's elect, strangers in the world, scattered throughout Pontus, Galatia, Cappadocia, Asia and Bithynia, who have been chosen according to the foreknowledge of God the Father, through the sanctifying work of the Spirit, for obedience to Jesus Christ and sprinkling by his blood.
> Grace and peace be yours in abundance.
> Praise be to the God and Father of our Lord Jesus Christ! In his great mercy he has given us new birth into a living hope through the resurrection of Jesus Christ from the dead, and into an inheritance that can never perish, spoil or fade—kept in heaven for you, who through faith are shielded by God's power until the coming of the salvation that is ready to be revealed in the last time. In this you greatly rejoice,

though now for a little while you may have had to suffer grief in all kinds of trials. These have come so that your faith—of greater worth than gold, which perishes even though refined by fire—may be proved genuine and may result in praise, glory and honor when Jesus Christ is revealed. Though you have not seen him, you love him; and even though you do not see him now, you believe in him and are filled with an inexpressible and glorious joy, for you are receiving the goal of your faith, the salvation of your souls (1 Peter 1:1-9).

Jean's Release from Anger

Jean initially felt God had abandoned her and that He had particularly abandoned Greg in his illness. Prior to Greg's suicide, Jean thought she understood that God doesn't always heal people on earth but sometimes allows them to suffer. After Greg's suicide, Jean's anger was intense. She couldn't understand why God allowed Greg to get to such a depth of despair that he killed himself.

It took Jean a few years to come to terms with how she felt. She argued with God and told Him about her anger through yelling, weeping, breaking dishes and glasses, and finally, by talking with a counselor. Although she still feels a level of distrust with the Lord, she has begun to feel His presence through mental pictures. The peace and love of the Lord is what melted her anger.

Linda's Antidote to Bitterness

Linda walks closely with Jesus and feels that she grieved Carl's death with victory because of her faith. She and Carl lived their lives with prayer and thanksgiving. While remembering the days prior to Carl's death, Linda recalled how God had provided a safe home as He prepared her to be alone. Linda and Carl had moved from a dangerous city to a safer, much smaller town a few months before Carl died. Although, as a new widow, Linda considered returning to her previous home, she was unable to get out of her lease in the new city and had to stay there. Linda believes that God's plan included her living in the new city so she would meet the man who became her new husband and a great stepdad for her two sons.

Carl died more than ten years ago. Linda still can't accept that it happened, but she believes that God uses our limited understanding of situations to get us through. Shortly after being widowed, Linda struggled with God because she was such a young mom with hopes and dreams that were gone the instant her husband fell into the Grand Canyon. However, she held on to God through prayer and worship, and tried to learn more about His Word. Rather than becoming bitter, she is drenched in God's Word and has a deep faith. Her spirit is so warm and welcoming that all who know Linda experience God's love.

Peace for Beverly

Once when Mark was sick, Beverly's phone rang at seven in the morning. The man on the other end of the phone was one of Mark's friends. He said that even though it was early, he felt that God had told him to call. In fact, this call came minutes after Mark had his second stroke and Beverly truly needed help. The friend's call was an answer to Beverly's prayer for help.

Beverly remembered Mark's death as meaningful. She and her daughter took turns staying by Mark's bedside round the clock. About one in the morning, Beverly took over for her daughter. She began reciting Psalm 23. When she got to "I will dwell in the house of the Lord forever" Mark breathed his last breath. Beverly took comfort in the thought that Mark had gone to be with the Lord forever.

Mark was tremendously handy around the house. Until his death, Beverly never had to perform household maintenance. After Mark was gone, Beverly tried to care for their beach house alone. She felt unable to do all that was needed and wanted reassurance that she was doing okay. Several months later, Beverly dreamed that she saw Mark sitting in a chair in her bedroom. In her dream, Mark didn't say a word while she poured out her heart to him concerning all of her worries. Then she began to feel peace in knowing that even though she wasn't doing things exactly as Mark would have, she was doing okay. Beverly believes that the Lord brought the peace of Philippians 4:7 which says, "And the peace of God, which transcends all understanding, will guard your hearts and your minds in Christ Jesus."

An Invisible Hug for Marcy

I relied very heavily on Jesus to take away my pain. After Jamie's death, the pain associated with his loss was so great that my crying was more like wailing. I simply couldn't seem to stop.

One morning I sat on the landing above the stairs as I cried for what seemed like a very long time. Finally, unable to catch my breath, I cried out to Jesus to take the pain away. Immediately I felt an arm going over my shoulders from the right shoulder to the left, as though someone was kneeling on my right side. The tears stopped. I had no pain, and I said "whoa" as I realized what was happening. I looked around, but of course saw no one there. I have no real explanation for this incident. However, I know that Jesus is alive and He cares about His children. "The Lord watches over the alien and sustains the fatherless and the widow" (Psalm 146:9).

Chapter Seven
Discussion Questions

1. What kind of conversations are you having with God now that the path is difficult?

2. What special times have you had with God?

3. Are you closer to or further away from God? Why?

Do you know Jesus as your Savior? If you answered "no" but you would like to know Him, please pray this simple prayer. "God, I want to be saved through your Son, Jesus. Jesus, I trust you to save me because you died on the cross for my sins. Please come into my life and forgive my sins."

If you prayed that prayer and want to talk to me about your decision, please go to my Web site, www.marcythecoach. com, and send me an e-mail telling me of your decision. I would love to hear from you.

Chapter Eight

The First Year

W hen your husband dies it is hard to think past the next fifteen minutes, let alone into the next week, month, or year. Even if we try, we cannot stop time. I understand feeling that there is no reason to go on. I understand how women die of broken hearts after their cherished husbands die. I understand wanting God to take you because the pain of loss is so great that you can hardly breathe. Yet, we must go on.

We have children or grandchildren who need the wisdom, love, and care only we can provide. We have jobs that give us reasons to get up and get dressed every morning. Although dying seems like the easiest solution to the pain, God has not yet called us. We ask, "Why?" We ask, "How?" We may be angry at God, at our husbands, or at the world in general, but we are still breathing and we have choices to make.

We can choose to wallow in our grief and let it pull us down like quicksand snuffing out our ability to make a difference in the lives of those we love, or we can choose life.

My "First-Year" Experiences

I have had two "first-year" experiences. Neal, my first husband, died September 13, 1984. At that time I was a part-time student. When Neal died, I pulled out of my classes for a semester since I knew I wouldn't be able to handle college, grieving, being a single mom, and all my other responsibilities.

Life began to get into a routine of Jayme's school, after-school sports, and homework. Then Thanksgiving and Christmas came. While Neal was alive, we had always visited my family in Pennsylvania over Thanksgiving, so that was what Jayme and I did again. There was an unspoken sadness over the holiday feast but we got through it. Sometimes just getting through a holiday is the best thing you can do. Christmas was much the same. We went through the motions of the holiday and persevered until it was over.

Jayme and I lived in an area of the United States which got a lot of snow. The winter after Neal died was particularly snowy and although I had a snow blower, I was afraid to use it. However, I had one special neighbor who always cleared my driveway. I found it interesting that Mr. Brown, my special neighbor, was one of the newest homeowners in the neighborhood. I had only met him and his wife a few times. In the beginning, I didn't even know who was clearing my driveway. Then one day I happened to catch him in the act. All these years later, I still remember Mr. Brown's kind actions.

After my second husband, Jamie, died I had another year of "firsts." This was the first time I had ever truly lived alone. Jamie died on my birthday in June of 2001. Six weeks after he died, my son, Jayme, married Megan, my beautiful daughter-in-law.

Three months later, on September 11, 2001, the day the planes hit the World Trade Center, I truly felt alone and frightened. Since I lived very close to Washington DC and the Pentagon, I wondered if I should sell my home and move to a more remote area for safety. I called a realtor in the tiny town where my parents and in-laws lived but ultimately, after spending a day looking at houses, I decided to stay in the house God had given me.

Again, the holidays were sad as we remembered previous Thanksgivings and Christmases. New Year's Eve could have been extremely bad except that the Lord provided a local party for me to attend. I left the party early and was in bed prior to midnight. Again, though, I still think so kindly of the couple who invited me to their party. I barely knew them and have seen them rarely since that occasion. They showed kindness to me at a time when I truly needed it.

Day-to-day Life in the First Year

Going through the routine you went through every day when your husband was alive will feel different now that he is gone. After my first husband died, I continued to cook because I knew my son needed to eat. Jayme and I kept to the routine of his sports and elementary school and my volunteer work and college classes. My need to nurture was fulfilled by being a mom. Sometimes Jayme would "take me out" to a local restaurant for dinner. Although I drove, he paid for our meal out of the allowance he had saved. I treasure the memory of those "dates."

Jamie and I always ate breakfast together. It was a special time for us where we discussed what we would do that day. After he died, I found that I needed to change what I ate for breakfast and the order in which I did things at the start of my day. I joined a gym and started working out first thing in the morning. When I returned from the gym, I got dressed for work, had breakfast, then headed out the door.

Coming home after work to an empty house was normal for me because I had always gotten home first when Jamie was alive. However, my routine after arriving home from work was very different. By this time my son had moved out and I didn't have to cook dinner for anyone but myself. Since I don't like to cook and I view cooking as a nurturing experience, when there was no one to nurture, I didn't cook. The thought of cooking for only me was so painful that I simply avoided it. I did get hungry and I did gain weight so I know I was eating, but food was unimportant to me.

Some women enjoy the experience of cooking and I would encourage them to continue cooking but to do so in smaller quantities. Putting on weight is easy when you have no one watching how much you eat.

Every Minute, Every Hour, Every Day

What if you don't have a job to keep you busy? My suggestion is, think about something you always wanted to do but have never done and make arrangements to do it. Continually, day after day, sitting alone in your home reading or watching TV is just not mentally or physically healthy. Although you may THINK you are fine, depression can sneak in without your knowing it. Go out with friends, find an exercise or craft class that you like, join a book club or Bible study. Volunteer at your church or with an organization whose ideas you support. PLEASE DO SOMETHING that gets you out of the house where you will laugh and interact with others.

Memory Lapse and Fog

Recent widows are often confused. Certain words won't come to their minds. They are forgetful and they can become frustrated with themselves due to the inability to be as sharp as they once were. This is usually a stress-related condition which will eventually go away.

I remember going into a gym where a woman gave me a tour of the facility. I left the gym to think about whether or not I wanted to join. When I returned to the gym the next day, I was not sure that the woman who greeted me was the same one who had given me the tour. She was insulted that I did not remember her, but I knew that this was just another example of the confusion I was experiencing.

During the months after each of my husbands died, I had to give myself quite a bit of grace and ask for grace from others because I truly was living in a fog. For someone who usually has a quick, clear mind, living in a fog is very frustrating. My fog did not lift for several months. Then one day I realized that I was able to think more clearly. I cannot say that I did anything to go from the fog to clarity, but I think a combination of time and doing grief work helped.

Volunteering

During my lifetime, I have spent more hours doing volunteer work than paid work. Some of my jobs were more fulfilling than others. Over time, I realized that when I agreed to spend my time volunteering for an organization, I needed to come away feeling good about the experience or it wasn't worth my time. I have had volunteer jobs where I worked with a few other women doing a task that allowed us to talk while we worked. This type of volunteer activity was a win-win situation. The organization got their job completed and I enjoyed interacting with other people. During other volunteer situations I have found myself in a corner or cubicle doing some sort of mindless task. Those volunteer situations were far from personally fulfilling and I usually went home feeling worse than before I left because I had no people contact.

When you volunteer, don't accept a task that puts you off in a corner sorting papers or stamping envelopes by yourself. Ask to have a task that puts you in contact with others. If the organization doesn't have jobs that fulfill your needs, go to another organization. It is important to do volunteer work that makes you feel good when you are finished.

Social Invitations

For a while, people who care about you will call daily or weekly. They will stop by and invite you to go places. But, if you decline their invitations over and over, they will stop calling and you will be alone. Only *you* can decide what your life will be like from this point on. If you want to have a full life with friends, you must be a friend. If you want to be around people, you must be fun to have around. It is your life and your choice.

Dating can happen when you are ready for it. Although you may have only been single for a few months, if someone asks you to go on a date and you want to go, I recommend that you go. Please don't worry about what the neighbors will think or that you have abandoned your deceased spouse's memory because you choose to go on a date. Unless someone has walked in your shoes, they will never understand exactly how you feel or what you are thinking. I applaud you for realizing that you must continue to live.

Every widow with whom I spoke mentioned how hard it was to get through the first year after her husband died. When you are a widow, you have to do all the things your husband used to do for you. You will have to take out the trash, make the bank deposits, write the checks, get the car inspected, pay the taxes, remember everyone's birthday, fix whatever breaks, change the heater filters, and on and on it goes. Can you do it? Yes, you can. Will it be fun? Probably not. Will you be stronger at the end of the first year? Definitely yes.

Through all of our pain, Jean, Beverly, Lori, Flo, Linda, Debby, and I all chose to leave tracks of joy and sunshine. Debby, Jean, Beverly, and Lori have chosen to remain single while Flo, Linda, and I have remarried. Whether or not you remarry, you will impact those around you in some way. My hope is that you will be remembered for persevering through the painful stage of loss to the destination of joy.

Chapter Eight
Discussion Questions

1. If you are past the one-year anniversary of your spouse's death, what were your first-year experiences? If you are still in your first year, you may want to reflect on the year so far and write your thoughts for future reflection.

2. Who has helped you along the way?

3. What are your unmet needs? How can you get those needs met?

4. Where are you in the first-year healing process?

Chapter Nine

My Final Thoughts

Death changes us. It brings pain, disillusionment, and experiences we never wanted in our lives. Each widow mentioned in my book realized that there was more to be done in her life after her world collapsed. In her need to move forward, she asked, "What do I do now?" Doing "something" is the first step toward moving *through* the pain and fog into the new life waiting in the distance. The operative word here is *through*. Those who choose to stop with the identity of "widow" don't move through, but only move around inside the pain, fear, and fog.

Being a widow need not be your destination in life; it can be only a *stage*. If you list all the things you are in life, like daughter, sister, mother, career woman, child of God, neighbor, friend, homeowner or renter, and so forth, you will see that "widow" is only a small part of the larger picture of who you really are. All of the good times and hard times have been integrated to make up the total "you." We choose how we view our lives. We can truly go from sorrow to dancing. We are victims or we are overcomers. I have chosen to overcome. What is your choice?

Psalm 30:10-12

"Hear, O Lord, and be merciful to me;
O Lord, be my help."
You turned my wailing into dancing;
you removed my sackcloth and clothed me with joy,
that my heart may sing to you and not be silent.
O Lord my God, I will give you thanks forever.

Epilogue

When my first husband died I was attending a community college to receive my associate's degree in computer science. I completed that degree prior to moving to Maryland with my second husband, Jamie. While married to Jamie I received my bachelor of arts degree in psychology with a concentration in human resources.

As I grieved Jamie's death, I wondered what I should do with the rest of my life. I had always been the one to whom women came with their questions about life. One day, a friend asked what I was passionate about. I really had to think hard to answer.

I finally answered that I loved mentoring women. He asked more questions and then announced, "That's coaching!" I had never even heard of coaching. This friend gave me several Web sites where I could find out more about coaching.

I eagerly started the search and became very excited about what I found. I knew that I had indeed found my passion. Already on my bookshelves were fifty-three books which could be used as references for my coaching practice. God had again prepared the way.

I went to seminars and workshops about coaching where I heard about Transformational Leadership Coaching (now called Life Forming Coaching). I became a certified coach through TLC and have had a thriving coaching practice since 2002. Coaching is done over the phone, so my clients can be located anywhere in the United States.

My passion is to help all women: widowed, divorced, or those who just want to set their next goal to thrive, not just survive.

If you would like to talk about your life, please contact me
at
www.marcythecoach.com or 703-725-2333

I am here to help you.

Marcy

Appendix

Action Steps to Move through Loss

Journal your thoughts

Ask for help and accept help

Be around caring people and allow them to comfort you

Give yourself and others grace to make mistakes

Join a grief group and share your story

Exercise

Cry

Put off making big decisions for at least a year

Forgive those who have hurt you

Do a personal check concerning your attitude. Are you bitter? If so, learn to forgive

Thank those who have helped you

Plan activities and remain engaged in life

Realize that you are not alone. God is always present

Have fun . . . try dancing!

My Journal